Tom Petty Biogra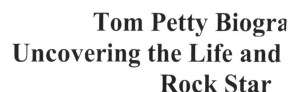
Uncovering the Life and
Rock Star

"MUSIC IS PROBABLY THE ONLY REAL MAGIC I HAVE ENCOUNTERED IN MY LIFE. THERE'S NOT SOME TRICK INVOLVED WITH IT. IT'S PURE AND IT'S REAL. IT MOVES, IT HEALS, IT COMMUNICATES AND DOES ALL THESE INCREDIBLE THINGS"

- Tom Petty -

By Joshua Michael Greene

TABLE OF CONTENTS

Tom Petty Biography

Many individuals find it difficult to cope with the passing of a beloved musician like Tom Petty. Legendary musicians such as Tom Petty, Elvis Presley, George Michael, and Bob Marley have affected countless people's lives and souls. Their ability to share their musical abilities and, at times, their personal lives with their fans was a great gift. Regrettably, unfortunate circumstances, accidents, or health concerns steal great musicians away from their family and fans much too soon. Every great song ultimately fades away, but is that any excuse not to appreciate the music? Tom Petty was an incredible artist who pulled in his admirers with his love of life, music, and people.

Early Life and Birth

Earl and Kitty Petty's eldest son, Thomas Earl Petty, was born on October 20, 1950 in Gainesville, Florida. Tom has a younger brother named Bruce. In interviews, Petty frequently mentioned that he had a close relationship with his mother. Petty was at the pinnacle of his popularity when his mother died on October 21, 1980, yet her tragedy had a significant impact on him.

Regrettably, the same cannot be true about his relationship with his father. Petty and his father did not have a love relationship, and Petty has said that it was abusive, both physically and verbally. Petty was also close to his younger brother, although it is unknown if his younger brother suffered as a result of his father's connection with him. Petty and his father did not have a love relationship, and Petty has said that it was abusive, both physically and verbally.

Petty was also close to his younger brother, although it is unknown if his sibling experienced the same harsh behavior from their father. Following years of torture, Petty found sanctuary in music and chose to explore where it would take him. His father was quite critical of his musical interests. Petty stated in interviews over the years that his father believed his love of music and the arts was undesirable. He disagreed with Petty's decision to continue his career as a musician. Earl Petty died on December 10, 1999, without entirely resolving his disagreements with his son. With his admiration for renowned performers like Elvis Presley, Petty's passion in music grew, and he decided it was time to learn to play the guitar.

Petty met Elvis Presley on the set of his film, Follow That Dream, when he was just ten years old. This life-changing encounter was a godsend that would open many possibilities for Petty. Petty was also a tremendous fan of The Beatles and their incredible musical abilities. Petty's passion for music was profoundly impacted by the 1960s, when garage bands were making a big mark in the music industry.

Petty was a bass guitarist for the band Epics throughout his high school years. At the age of 17, he had concluded that school was not for him and had quit out. He collected his musically oriented buddies and formed Mudcrutch, in which he was the bass player and lead man.

Bands' Music Career

"I'LL KEEP THIS WORLD FROM DRAGGIN' ME DOWN. GONNA STAND MY GROUND. AND I WON'T BACK DOWN"

The Epics were Petty's first band, which he joined in 1970. Later that year, Petty and fellow band member Tom Leadon decided to form Mudcrutch. Petty and Leadon, Jim Lenehan, Randall Marshall, and Mike Campbell were among the five members. Petty's primary preoccupation in the band was the vocals and bass. He worked tirelessly with his band to perfect their sound. Lenehan and Leadon left the band in 1972, and were replaced by Danny Roberts and Benmont Tech. Mudcrutch were frequently seen performing at Gainesville's Dub's Club. Before all the fame and fanfare, this club was where Petty's initial admirers could see him in action. Mudcrutch chose to sign with Shelter Records and relocate to Los Angeles in 1974. However, their debut song, "Depot Street," was a flop, and their band gradually disbanded. By the end of 1975, Mudcrutch had been disbanded by their label, and everyone had gone their own ways. In 2007, Petty believed it would be a fantastic idea to re-create an album with some of the original band members. Band members Tom Leadon, Randall Marsh, Mike Campbell, and Benmont Tech collaborated with Petty to make two incredible albums. They went on concert tours and ended their last show together in 2016.

<Mudcrutch's Childhood>

Tom Petty was a member of the band Mudcrutch before becoming famous with the Heartbreakers. In the early 1970s, the band was founded in Gainesville, Florida, with Petty on lead vocals and guitar, Mike Campbell on lead guitar, Tom Leadon on rhythm guitar, Randall Marsh on drums, and Benmont Tench on keyboards.

Mudcrutch immediately became popular in their local music scene, performing a combination of original songs and covers at local clubs and bars. Their sound was influenced by traditional rock & roll, with an emphasis on catchy tunes and strong musicianship.

Mudcrutch moved to Los Angeles in 1974 in search of a record deal. They were unable to find success in the very competitive music market, and the band separated after a few years.

Despite their brief existence, Mudcrutch had a lasting impact on Petty's musical career. His later work with the Heartbreakers would be influenced by the band's sound and approach, and several of their songs would be re-recorded and published on later albums.

Petty reunited with several of his former Mudcrutch bandmates, including Campbell, Tench, and Marsh, in 2008 to record a self-titled Mudcrutch album. The album was a commercial and critical success, demonstrating the band's continued relevance and impact on Petty's music.

Mudcrutch is still a vital part of Tom Petty's early music career, and the band's history is recognized by fans and musicians all over the world. Mudcrutch had a vital role in defining Petty's musical identity and paving the route for his eventual success, from their humble origins in Gainesville to their reunion decades later.

<Heartbreakers>

With the demise of Mudcrutch in 1976, Tom Petty helped form Tom Petty and the Heartbreakers. Following Blair's departure, Howie Epstein and Scott Thurston were added to the group. The band quickly gained popularity in the rock and roll community. The band had signed with Shelter Label, and their debut album sold a staggering number of units worldwide. It wasn't long before the band began releasing record after album. Their music was so popular that their admirers couldn't get enough of it. "Breakdown," "American Girl," "Listen to Her Heart," and "Refugee" are among the band's finest hits. It wasn't long after the success of their debut record that this incredible band realized that traveling the country was necessary. Over their career, Tom Petty and the Heartbreakers received several honors and nominations. The band was chosen to perform at the Super Bowl XLII Halftime Show in 2008. Most of Tom Petty's band mates were claimed to have been by his hospital bedside as he breathed his final breath after learning of his deadly heart arrest. Although the band has not formally chosen to disband, Tom Petty and the Heartbreakers remaining together following Petty's death appears unlikely. Petty's last tour with the Heartbreakers ended on September 25, 2017, for the band's official 40th Anniversary Tour of the United States. Petty would be killed by a heart attack less than two weeks later.

During his solo success and his tenure with the Heartbreakers, Petty formed the Traveling Wilburys. Tom Petty, Bob Dylan, George Harrison, Jeff Lynne, and Roy Orbison were among the musicians in the band. This outstanding band released two excellent albums. The band was never expected to be a success in the music industry, yet they immediately became a smash and went on to win Grammy Awards. Petty discovered that playing with his buddies was quite relaxing and therapeutic for his stressful profession. The songs on their albums were written and produced by all of the band members. Regrettably, Roy Orbison died in 1988, thus he missed the release of the band's second album. Although the Flying Wilburys never made their live debut, they made up for it with smash singles like "Handle with Care," "She's My Baby," and "Tweeter and the Monkey Man."

Tom Petty released many albums throughout his career, both as a solo artist and with his band Tom Petty and the Heartbreakers.

Tom Petty and the Heartbreakers were still a relatively obscure band in the late 1970s, attempting to build a reputation for themselves in the extremely competitive music industry. It all changed in 1979, with the publication of their third album, "Damn the Torpedoes."

The album was a commercial and critical success, solidifying Petty's place as a rock and roll legend. It featured popular singles including "Don't Do Me Like That" and "Refugee," both of which charted in the top 40 on the Billboard Hot 100. The album's success was owed in great part to Petty's songwriting abilities, as well as the Heartbreakers' superb musicianship.

Nonetheless, the production of "Damn the Torpedoes" was not without its difficulties. Petty and his record label, MCA, were at odds over contractual difficulties while the album was recorded. Petty had refused to sign a long-term deal with MCA, so the label withheld the master tapes for "Damn the Torpedoes" until he agreed to their requirements.

Despite this setback, Petty and the Heartbreakers stayed committed to creating the finest album they could. They collaborated with producer Jimmy Iovine to create a sound that was both raw and refined, with catchy songs and memorable lyrics that would connect with fans.

When the record was ultimately released, it was a huge hit. It peaked at number two on the Billboard 200, selling nearly four million copies in the United States alone. The album was acclaimed as a masterpiece by critics, who praised its intensity, emotion, and musicality.

The popularity of "Damn the Torpedoes" elevated Tom Petty and the Heartbreakers from cult beloved to one of the world's biggest bands. They went on a big tour to promote the album, performing sold-out gigs to loving fans all over the world.

Petty and the Heartbreakers continued to generate successful albums and hit songs in the years that followed, solidifying their position as one of the greatest rock and roll bands of all time. Yet, it was "Damn the Torpedoes" that launched them to success, and it remains one of the most revered and influential albums in rock & roll history.

Tom Petty and the Heartbreakers:

- Tom Petty and the Heartbreakers (1976)
- You're Gonna Get It! (1978)
- Damn the Torpedoes (1979)
- Hard Promises (1981)
- Long After Dark (1982)
- Southern Accents (1985)
- Let Me Up (I've Had Enough) (1987)
- Into the Great Wide Open (1991)
- Echo (1999)
- The Last DJ (2002)
- Mojo (2010)
- Hypnotic Eye (2014)

During his career, Tom Petty maintained a strong friendship with the members of the Heartbreakers. Many of them had been playing music together since Mudcrutch, and they had a deep musical and emotional affinity.

Mike Campbell, the Heartbreakers' guitarist, was a particularly essential collaborator for Petty. Many of Petty's biggest successes were co-written by the two, including "Refugee," "Don't Do Me Like That," and "Free Fallin'." Campbell's distinctive guitar playing was an integral component of the Heartbreakers' sound, and he also made considerable contributions to Petty's solo work.

Another major collaborator for Petty was Benmont Tench, who played keyboards in the Heartbreakers. Tench's piano and organ skills contributed depth and texture to many of Petty's compositions, and he was also a songwriter and arranger.

Additional Heartbreakers members, such as Ron Blair (bass), Stan Lynch (drums), and Howie Epstein (bass), played significant parts in Petty's music over the years. Epstein was a crucial collaborator on Petty's solo albums, and he co-wrote several of his biggest songs, including "Free Fallin'" and "I Won't Back Down."

Despite various differences and tensions over the years, Petty and the Heartbreakers remained close friends and collaborators until his death. Their music continues to inspire and influence musicians all over the world, and their reputation as one of the greatest rock and roll bands of all time is unshakeable.

Career in Solo Music

Tom Petty had a successful solo career as well. In 1989, he released his debut solo album, "Full Moon Fever," which was a huge commercial success. Hit songs from the album were "Free Fallin'," "I Won't Back Down," and "Runnin' Down a Dream."

Petty's solo work displayed his songwriting abilities and allowed him to experiment with many musical styles. "Wildflowers," his second solo album, was published in 1994 and received critical acclaim for its thoughtful and sensitive songs.

Petty continues to release solo albums while touring and recording with the Heartbreakers over the years. His solo recordings have gained critical acclaim, including "Highway Companion" (2006) and "Hypnotic Eye" (2014).

Throughout his career, Petty collaborated with numerous musicians in addition to his solo work. He collaborated on multiple occasions with Stevie Nicks, including the hit ballad "Stop Draggin' My Heart Around" from her 1981 album "Bella Donna." Over the years, he has also worked with Johnny Cash, Jeff Lynne, and many other performers.

Petty's solo work gave him the opportunity to express his originality and demonstrate his versatility as a musician. His admirers respected him for his ability to connect with them through his lyrics, and his music was noted for its emotional depth and strong narrative.

Tom Petty died in 2017, but his impact as a solo artist and rock legend goes on. He created a legacy of music that continues to inspire and influence musicians today, and his songs will be recognized as some of the best in rock and roll history.

Tom Petty solo:

-   Full Moon Fever (1989)
-   Wildflowers (1994)
-   Highway Companion (2006)

Tom Petty also released several live albums and compilation albums over the years. Some notable ones include "Pack Up the Plantation: Live!" (1985), "Playback" (1995), and "The Live Anthology" (2009). Petty was also a member of the supergroup The Traveling Wilburys, which released two albums in the late 1980s.

Side Projects and Collaborations

Tom Petty was known throughout his career for his collaborations and side projects, which allowed him to experiment with numerous musical styles and work with a wide range of musicians. Among his most notable collaborations are:

Petty was a member of the Traveling Wilburys, a supergroup that featured George Harrison, Bob Dylan, Jeff Lynne, and Roy Orbison. The band issued two albums in the late 1980s, showing their collective talents and bringing together some of rock and roll's biggest personalities.

Stevie Nicks: On multiple occasions, Petty collaborated with Stevie Nicks, including the hit track "Stop Draggin' My Heart Around" from her 1981 album "Bella Donna." They had a tight personal and professional relationship, and their collaborations resulted in some of the era's most iconic and adored songs.

Johnny Cash: On multiple occasions, Petty collaborated with Johnny Cash, including the duet "The Running Kind" from Cash's album "Unchained." They each admired each other's music, and their partnerships were distinguished by mutual respect and friendliness.

Petty worked on various side projects with his band, the Heartbreakers, in addition to his collaborations with other musicians. These ventures included the album "The Traveling Wilburys Vol. 3," which featured several Heartbreakers members, as well as the soundtrack for the film "She's the One," which Petty and the Heartbreakers recorded.

Petty's collaborations and side ventures allowed him to experiment with numerous musical styles and collaborate with some of the music industry's top personalities. They also demonstrated his musical diversity and willingness to take risks and explore new things.

The Superstardom of the 1980s

Tom Petty and the Heartbreakers saw a boom in popularity in the early 1980s, catapulting them to superstardom. Their 1979 album "Damn the Torpedoes" was a great commercial success, containing smash singles like "Refugee" and "Don't Do Me Like That."

Throughout the 1980s, Petty and the Heartbreakers continued to release successful albums and songs, cementing their reputation as one of rock and roll's most influential bands. They had a string of hits, including "Hard Promises" (1981), "Long After Dark" (1982), and "Southern Accents" (1985), which produced the hit single "Don't Come Around Here No More."

Petty's success during this time period was owed in part to his ability to adjust his sound to the changing musical landscape. He blended aspects of new wave and punk into his music to create a sound that was both timeless and modern.

Petty's success in the 1980s was further aided by his music videos, which became a popular medium for marketing his music and extending his fan base. His legendary videos, like "Don't Come

Around Here No More" and "Free Fallin'," were MTV favorites that helped solidify his place in pop culture lore.

Despite commercial success, Petty maintained his artistic vision and personal integrity. In the face of commercial pressures, he refused to compromise his ideals or his music, and he remained true to himself and his followers throughout his meteoric journey to superstardom.

The impact of Tom Petty's success in the 1980s can still be felt today. His music has become ingrained in the cultural environment, influencing and inspiring future generations of musicians and listeners. And his dedication to sincerity and artistic integrity continues to serve as an example for artists of all genres and mediums.

Personal Interests and Acting Career

"MOST THINGS I WORRY ABOUT NEVER HAPPEN ANYWAY."

Petty, like his favorite rock and roll singer, Elvis Presley, participated in movies with minor roles or cameos. In 1978, he made his debut appearance on the big screen in the film FM. FM was a music-themed film with great actors like Michael Brandon and Cassie Yates. Petty was employed as a live performance artist in the film, which helped propel his musical career to new heights. Petty appeared on the television series It's Garry Shandling's Show and Made in Heaven between 1987 and 1990. Petty's major break in the film business came in 1997, when he played the mayor in Kevin Costner's The Postman. Petty was also given the opportunity to voice characters in The Simpsons and King of the Hill. His acting career was never as successful as his musical career, but Petty relished his time in front of the camera.

Petty, like any great musician, wanted to buy new instruments for his own personal and private usage. Guitars were his favorite instrument, and he possessed more than a dozen during his life. Petty was a guitar enthusiast, and his most renowned instruments were in steady use throughout his career. Petty's favorite instruments were a 1964 Fender Stratocaster that he used frequently during his early musical career and a 1965 Rose Morris guitar. Petty also assisted in the design and production of his own personal guitar, the Rickenbacker 660/12TP, which also bore Petty's signature.

Sirius XM chose to create a radio station in 2015 as a homage to Tom Petty's excellent music, branding it Tom Petty Radio. Listeners from all around the country may listen in and hear all of Tom's greatest hits.

Petty is also well-known in the artistic control and artistic freedom communities. He thought that every musician should be able to manage their own music and image. He was an excellent champion for our community, always standing out for their rights. When Petty was involved in a court issue over his songs in 1979, he founded this community. Petty has frequently spotted parallels between his work and the work of others, and owing to his thoroughness, he was able to prevent the production of some of the songs. Petty's unexpected declaration of bankruptcy in 1979 harmed both his self-esteem and his musical career. Petty learnt and matured as an artist from his early failures, and he utilized his expertise to educate other artists throughout the years.

Tom Petty had a variety of personal interests and hobbies in addition to his music career. He was an ardent reader who specialized in science fiction and fantasy books. He also enjoyed cars and was well-known for his collection of vintage vehicles.

Petty was also interested in film and television, and he appeared in a number of films and television shows throughout his career. His film credits include a cameo in "Made in Heaven" (1987) and a starring role in "The Postman" (1997). He also appeared on TV shows such as "The Simpsons," "King of the Hill," and "The Larry Sanders Show."

Petty's acting career demonstrated his adaptability and willingness to attempt new things. He approached his acting assignments with the same enthusiasm and dedication that he did his music, and his fans admired his willingness to venture outside of his comfort zone and take on new challenges.

Despite his popularity as an actor, Petty remained committed to his music business. He toured and recorded with the Heartbreakers until his death in 2017, and his music is a monument to his talent and love of rock and roll.

<Acting Career>

Tom Petty was recognized for his forays into acting and his personal interests outside of music, in addition to his music career. Among his significant acting roles are:

He played the Angel of Music in the 1987 film "Made in Heaven."
The 1987 television show "It's Garry Shandling's Show," in which he portrayed himself.

In the 1997 film "The Postman," he played the Mayor of Bridge City. While Petty's acting career was brief, it exhibited his artist's adaptability and eagerness to take on new projects.

<Personal Interests>

Petty was known in his personal life for his love of cars and motorcycles, and he was an obsessive collector of antique vehicles. He also enjoyed art and was known to collect pieces by modern artists such as Shepard Fairey and Banksy.

Petty was also a staunch supporter of independent musicians and composers and a passionate campaigner for artists' rights. He was a strong opponent of the commercial methods of the music industry and campaigned fiercely for artists' rights to manage their own creative output.

Petty was a dedicated husband and father in addition to his music and activism, and his personal integrity and compassion left an indelible mark on those who knew him. His legacy as an artist and as a person is still being acknowledged by fans and musicians all across the world.

Private Life

Petty did not have the ideal upbringing, but he was determined that if he were given the opportunity to have children, their childhoods would be vastly different from his. Petty realized from an early age that he was in love and wanted to marry. Petty's first marriage to childhood sweetheart Jane Benyo terminated suddenly due to his turbulent upbringing and youth. Petty and Benyo met when they were just 17 years old and decided to live together soon after. Petty and Benyo married on March 31, 1974, and their marriage lasted 22 years until their divorce in 1996. Petty and Benyo have two children, Adria and AnnaKim Violette, from their marriage. Addiction to narcotics was one of the ongoing challenges that both Petty and Benyo faced during their marriage. Benyo, too, tumbled down the rabbit hole when she developed alcoholism. In contrast to how he was reared, Petty was devoted to his girls. As his girls grew and matured, they noted that their father's attention and affection were pure, but their mother was more verbally aggressive than she should have been at times. Petty has frequently remarked that it was tough to preserve the peace throughout his marriage to Benyo owing to her developing mental condition and drug/alcohol usage. After his divorce from Benyo, Petty fell into a deep pit of heroin addiction, but he credits his second wife's love and support for helping him overcome his terrible habit.

In 1991, Petty married his second wife, Dana York. Petty was still married to Benyo at the time, while York was still married to her first husband. Despite widespread conjecture, Petty and York maintained that they only got romantically linked after being separated from their significant others. On June 3, 2001, Petty and York married in Las Vegas. They chose to celebrate their love in private, but had a modest ceremony for their closest relatives and friends a week later. Petty has frequently stated that York would urge him to go to counseling and accompany him to sessions to help him conquer his addictions. Dylan, Petty's stepson from York's first marriage, was considered a son by Petty. Petty is also a grandfather who enjoys being involved in the lives of his grandchildren.

Apart from his children, Benyo and York, Petty had other important women in his life. Stevie Nicks was a crucial part of Petty's boyhood and remained a lifelong buddy. They met in 1978 and quickly clicked because they both loved music. Nicks went on to become a fantastic solo performer as well as a member of Fleetwood Mac. The couple discovered that their passion for music was so strong that they needed to collaborate on a duet. Their debut duet was on the song "Insider" in 1981. "Needles and Pins," published in 1986, was another of their hit duets. Despite the fact that Petty and Nicks worked closely together, their connection was never more than a friendship. A misunderstanding chat with Petty's first wife, Benyo, inspired one of Nicks' finest compositions. According to the account, Nicks asked Benyo when she and Petty first met, and Benyo replied, "at the age of 17," which Nicks misheard as "at the edge of 17." Nicks was so taken with the sound and meaning of that line that she requested if she may use it in a song. Once Nicks penned the incredible song "Edge of Seventeen," with lyrics closely echoing Petty and Benyo's lives, the rest is history. Petty and Nicks shared a great deal of respect and affection for one another. Despite their friendship, neither Nicks nor Petty could have predicted Petty's addiction to heroin and marijuana. In an interview, she claimed, "I would never guess, not in a million years, that Tom Petty would start taking heroin." Thankfully for Tom, his second wife would pick up the pieces and put him back on track. Stevie Nicks was devastated by the death of her good friend Petty. Fortunately, she may find calm and relaxation in the music the team has created over the years.

George Harrison, a member of the Beatles, was another close buddy of Petty's. This friendship appeared to surprise followers of both musicians because the two rarely discussed their relationship. Only years after Harrison's death in 2001 would Petty come honest about their friendship. Because the Beatles were such a big part of the music world and Petty's youth, he didn't want to brag about his connection with Harrison, so he kept it hidden. His connection with Harrison was developed even more when they formed the band Traveling Wilburys together. Petty was taken aback by Harrison's death, and the loss of such a close friend grieved him.

Petty has previously stated that he was a major supporter of Transcendental Meditation and practiced it on a regular basis. This sort of meditation has the advantage of clearing the mind and spirit of any undesirable bad energy.

In the late spring of 1987, one of Petty's detractors got the better of him and set fire to his home in Encino, California. Despite the fact that the most of the damage occurred in the basement and other areas of his home, Petty was able to recover the majority of his items and no one was injured.

Personal Struggles and Challenges

Tom Petty had a multitude of personal hardships and challenges throughout his life and career, despite his success as a singer. Petty's journey was punctuated by highs and lows that tested his fortitude and strength, from addiction to legal challenges.

Addiction was one of Petty's major issues. He suffered with substance abuse for many years before entering treatment in the 1990s to address his drug and alcohol problems. He was candid about his drug troubles, and he used music to cope with the difficulties he faced.

Another significant obstacle for Petty was his continuous legal disputes with MCA, his record label. Petty had declined to sign a long-term deal with the label in the early 1980s, resulting in a lengthy court struggle over the rights to his work. The disagreement was finally settled out of court, but it had a significant impact on Petty's professional and personal life.

Petty also struggled with personal issues in his relationships. In the late 1990s, he went through a painful divorce that left him mentally drained and unable to cope. He later remarried, but the experience stayed with him and influenced his work.

Despite these obstacles, Petty stayed committed to his music, producing some of the most memorable songs in rock & roll history. He was inspired by his personal problems, and his songs frequently tackled themes of loss, addiction, and salvation.

Petty faced another huge difficulty in his latter years when he was diagnosed with emphysema and other health difficulties. Despite his health issues, he continued to tour and play, but he was forced to cancel several events owing to his condition.

Petty remained a revered and respected figure in the music business throughout it all. His followers respected him for his candor, tenacity, and uncompromising devotion to his work. Notwithstanding his personal troubles and challenges, Tom Petty's position as one of rock and roll's greatest artists is solid, and his music continues to inspire and influence musicians worldwide.

Awards

"YOU BELONG SOMEWHERE YOU FEEL FREE."

Tom Petty's musical prowess earned him several prizes during his career. Tom Petty gained major distinctions and prizes as a solo artist, and he was also nominated for several awards while in a band. Despite the fact that Mudcrutch was the Pettys' first formal band, they received no awards, honors, or nominations during their time together. Petty has frequently stated that his time with this band was his "crutch" at the start of his career. Petty won multiple honors as a solo artist, including the following: "You Don't Know How It Feels" won Best Male Video at the 1995 MTV Video Music Awards, and Best Rock Vocal Performance-Male at the 1996 Grammy Awards. The Legend Award at the 2003 Radio Music Awards and the Billboard Century Award in 2005 Petty received several honors as an accomplice or band member for his great talent, including the following: Tom Petty and the Heartbreakers won Best Special Effects for "Don't Come Around Here No More" at the 1985 MTV Video Music Awards. The Traveling Wilburys won the Grammy Award for Best Rock Vocal Performance by a Duo or Group in 1990 for this album Traveling Wilburys Vol. 1. 1994 MTV Video Music Awards for Best Male Video for "Mary Jane's Last Dance" with Tom Petty and the Heartbreakers, and 2009 Grammy Award for Best Music Video, Long Form for "Runnin Down a Dream" with Tom Petty and the Heartbreakers.

Petty was appreciative of all of the outstanding accolades and distinctions bestowed upon him during his lifetime. Petty was endowed with remarkable skill, which allowed him to be nominated for the following prizes as a solo artist: Album of the Year for "Full Moon Fever" in 1990, and Best Rock Vocal Performance-Male for "Free Fallin" in 1991. "Learning to Fly" won the Grammy Award for Best Rock Song in 1992. Wildflowers won the Grammy Award for Best Rock Album in 1996. "Square One" won the Grammy Award for Best Song Written for a Motion Picture, Television, or Other Visual Media in 2006. (Elizabethtown), Highway Companion won the 2007 Grammy Award for Best Rock Album and the 2007 Grammy Award for Best Solo Rock Vocal Performance for "Saving Grace." Petty was nominated for the following prizes as a member of a band: Stevie Nicks and Tom Petty and the Heartbreakers won the 1982 Grammy Award for Best Rock Performance by a Duo or Group with Vocal for "Stop Draggin My Heart Around." Tom Petty and the Heartbreakers won the 1985 MTV Music Video Award for Video of the Year, Viewer's Choice, Best Direction, and Best Concept Video for "Don't Come Around Here No More." The Traveling Wilburys won the 1989 MTV Music Video Award for Best Group Video for "Handle with Care." Traveling Wilburys Vol. 1 received the 1990 American Music Awards for Favorite Pop/Rock New Artist. The Traveling Wilburys won the Grammy Award for Album of the Year in 1990 for Traveling Wilburys Vol. 1. "Into the Big Wide Open"

won the Grammy Award for Best Rock Performance by a Duo or Group in 1992. MTV Music Video Award for Best Male Video for "Into the Big Wide Open," co-written with Tom Petty and the Heartbreakers, in 1992. The song "My Back Pages," performed with Bob Dylan, Roger McGuinn, Eric Clapton, George Harrison, and Neil Young, won the Grammy Award for Best Rock Performance by a Duo or Group with Vocal in 1994. 1999 Grammy Award for Best Rock Single for "Room at the Top" with Tom Petty and the Heartbreakers, and 1999 Grammy Award for Best Rock Album for Echo with Tom Petty and the Heartbreakers, Mojo received a Grammy Award for Best Rock Album in 2011 alongside Tom Petty and the Heartbreakers. Hypnotic Eye received a 2015 Grammy Award for Best Rock Album alongside Tom Petty and the Heartbreakers, and "Into the Big Wide Open" received a 2009 MTV Music Video Award for Best Video (which should have earned a moonman).

Tom Petty and the Heartbreakers were honored with a star on the Hollywood Walk of Fame in 1999. The Rock & Roll Hall of Fame inducted Petty as one of their great musicians in 2002. It was a wonderful honor for Petty as a rock and roll musician to be elected into this Hall of Fame, especially since it is the same accolade conferred upon one of his favorite childhood vocalists, Elvis Presley. Petty and his Heartbreakers bandmates were awarded the Keys to the City of Gainesville, Florida, Petty's hometown, in 2006. One of Petty's most recent accomplishments was being named MusiCares Person of the Year in 2017. The experience of being recognized with such a prestigious accolade absolutely humbled Petty. "I am so very delighted to be honored as the MusiCares Person of the Year," Petty said during his acceptance speech. I personally know several folks who have benefited from MusiCares...this is a great honor." Regrettably, Petty's untimely death has left a tremendous void in the music world, and while he will not be honored with another Grammy (until posthumously), his legacy will live on via his wonderful work.

Albums and singles that have achieved success

Tom Petty dedicated his whole career to singing and performing music in order to make others happy. Petty wrote at least ten albums with the Heartbreakers, three solo albums, two albums with The Traveling Wilburys, and two albums with his first band, The Mudcrutch, during his lifetime. He'd come a long way for the scrawny little boy who was in a garage band with a few mates. Petty's success in a band and as a solo artist far exceeded his own expectations. Petty's solo albums include the 1989 Full Moon Fever Album, which has 5x Platinum Certifications, the 1994 Wildflowers Album, which has 3x Platinum Certificates, and the 2006 Highway Companion Album, which has a Gold Certificate. As a member of The Traveling Wilburys, Petty recorded two new albums and a compilation album: 1988 Traveling Wilburys Vol. 1 (3x Platinum Certificate), 1990 Traveling Wilburys Vol. 3 (Platinum Certificate), and 2007 The Traveling Wilburys Collection (Gold Certificate). Petty and his band, as one of the original members of Mudcrutch, recorded two albums: Mudcrutch in 2008 and 2 in 2016. Throughout the majority of his musical career, Petty has been associated with the band Tom Petty and the Heartbreakers. Following the band's popularity, the following albums were released: 1976 Tom Petty and the Heartbreakers (Gold Certificate), 1978 You're Gonna Get It (Gold Certificate), 1979 Damn the Torpedoes (Triple Platinum Certificate), 1981 Hard Promises (Platinum Certificate), Long After Dark, which received a Gold Certified in 1982, and Southern Accents, which received a Platinum Certificate in 1985. Let Me Up (I've Had Enough), released in 1987, has a Platinum Certified. 1991's Into the Big Wide Open, which has received two Platinum Certifications, 1996 Tracks and music from the Gold-certified album "She's the One," 1999 Echo with a Gold Certificate The Last DJ was released in 2002, Mojo in 2010, and Hypnotic Eye in 2014.

Petty has also released several compilation and live CDs for his fans' enjoyment. As a solo artist and band member, Petty showed an obvious ability for releasing exceptional records into the music world that have stood the test of time. As a solo artist and band member, he is best known for the following singles: "American Girl" in 1977, "Listen to Her Heart" in 1978. 1980 ""Here Comes My Daughter," 1982; "Straight into Darkness," 1986; and "Needles and Pins" (with Stevie Nicks), 1989's "I Won't Back Down," 1990's "Learning to Fly," 1993's "Mary Jane's Final Dance," 1994's "You Don't Know How It Feels," 2002's "The Last DJ," 2006's "Saving Grace," 2014's "American Dream Plan B," and 2016's "The Woods." ". With a career as long as Petty's, it's tough to choose out his favorite songs or albums. His incredible ability may be observed throughout three decades, and his music will be shared with the world for the rest of time.

Death

"YOU AND I WILL MEET AGAIN. WHEN WE'RE LEAST EXPECTING IT. SOMEWHERE IN SOME FAR OFF PLACE. I WILL RECOGNIZE YOUR FACE. I WON'T SAY GOODBYE MY FRIEND. FOR YOU AND I WILL MEET AGAIN."

Petty was discovered fully unconscious at his home in California early on October 2, 2017. Petty had gone into cardiac arrest after being discovered unconscious and not breathing. After Petty was discovered, he was taken to UCLA Medical Center at Santa Monica Hospital. After enormous effort and commitment, the physicians and personnel at UCLA Medical Center were unable to save Petty's life any longer. Tragically, Petty died of a heart attack at the age of 66 on Monday, October 2, 2017. Tony Dimitriades, Petty's manager, made the formal announcement of his death. "On behalf of the Tom Petty family, we are heartbroken to announce the unexpected passing of our father, husband, brother, leader, and friend Tom Petty," Dimitriades said. His family, closest friends, and bandmates surrounding him. Tom Petty's death was utterly unexpected and shook the music world to its core. Numerous celebrities, fans, and other artists expressed their heartfelt condolences for the passing of a wonderful guy on social media. Several false stories circulated the internet before Petty's real death, claiming that he had already died. Petty's family and friends were devastated and angered that word of his death had spread throughout the internet when they were still expecting for a miracle recovery from Petty. Some of the claims came from media sites like TMZ, while others came from non-fans on Twitter. According to TMZ, his family decided to withdraw Tom Petty from life support at 3:30 p.m. on October 2nd owing to no brain activity. Several news agencies, including Entertainment Tonight and CBS News, reported that Petty died at 4 p.m. on October 2, 2017. Unfortunately, these allegations were absolutely false, and the revelation of a beloved artist's premature death stunned and saddened fans and family members of Petty. The coroner's office in Los Angeles performed a comprehensive autopsy on Petty, however it has been stated that the specific cause of death is still unknown. One of the possible contributing causes of Petty's death was his persistent smoking of cigarettes since he was 17 years old. The coroner's office has issued a formal request for a toxicology screening, but the findings may take at least two weeks to complete and send. The 2nd of October, 2017 was a terrible day for music fans all around the world, but Tom Petty's legacy will live on via his family, bandmates, and music.

Tom Petty was an average man with amazing gifts, which he generously shared with the world for more than three decades of his life. While his life was cut much too soon, his memory and songs will undoubtedly live on in the hearts of his followers forever. No one will ever be able to dim Tom Petty's memory, and it will be amplified for the entire world to appreciate long after his untimely death.

Remembering Tom Petty:
Tributes and Reflections

Tom Petty's death in 2017 shocked his fans and the music world as a whole. His death left a gap in the business that many have tried to fill, and his influence on rock and roll music is still felt today.

Upon his death, there was a flood of condolences and thoughts from musicians, fans, and industry insiders. Many of these tributes emphasized Petty's influence as a musician and composer, emphasizing his ability to connect with listeners on a deeply emotional level and craft songs that spoke to the human experience.

Others praised Petty's dedication to artistic integrity and reluctance to compromise his vision or ideals. They appreciated his candor, genuineness, and unwavering devotion to his profession.

One thing was evident throughout the tributes and reflections: Tom Petty's impact on the world of music was immense. He was a true original, a rock and roll star known for his music, his energy, and his dedication to greatness.

While people listen to Petty's songs and reflect on his legacy, it's evident that his impact will be felt for years to come. His music continues to inspire and unite people all over the world, and his place as one of the greatest artists in rock & roll history is certain.

Tom Petty's Impact on Rock and Roll Music

Tom Petty's music has had a deep influence on generations of musicians and fans alike. His songs were noted for their catchy choruses, dramatic storytelling, and emotional depth, and his lyrics addressed to a generation of listeners looking for purpose and connection in a fast changing world.

The universality of Petty's music was one of its defining characteristics. His music spoke to people of various ages, genders, and socioeconomic backgrounds. His themes of love, grief, and desire were universal, and his music connected with people in ways that few other artists have.

Another significant component of Petty's influence on rock and roll music was his dedication to honesty. He was noted for refusing to compromise his artistic vision or integrity, and he remained faithful to himself and his music despite financial pressures and industry expectations.

The wide range of performers that identify Petty as an inspiration demonstrates his influence on rock & roll music. Bands as disparate as the Foo Fighters, Pearl Jam, and Taylor Swift have all commented about how Petty's songs influenced their own careers and approaches to music.

In addition to his music, Petty was a vocal supporter of artists' rights and was well-known for his encouragement of independent musicians and composers. He was a strong opponent of the commercial methods of the music industry and campaigned fiercely for artists' rights to manage their own creative output.

Petty's influence on rock & roll music has only risen in the years after his death. His music continues to inspire and influence musicians all around the world, and his place as one of the greatest artists in rock & roll history is certain.

Later Life and Legacy

Tom Petty continued to tour and record with the Heartbreakers in his latter years, delivering many albums that were well-received by fans and critics alike. Despite having to cancel multiple gigs due to health issues, Petty remained dedicated to his music and his fans, and he continued to perform live until his death in 2017.

Petty's legacy as a musician and songwriter is secure, and his influence on the world of rock and roll music is still felt today. He was noted for his ability to write songs that were both popular and profound, with lyrics that were both relatable and deeply personal.

Over the years, his music has impacted innumerable artists, and his songs are still recorded by musicians of all genres and backgrounds. Petty's work is a treasured and enduring part of the rock and roll canon, from classic successes like "Free Fallin'" and "Refugee" to deeper cuts like "Wildflowers" and "The Last DJ."

Petty's influence extends beyond his songs. He was an outspoken supporter of independent musicians and composers and a fervent campaigner for artists' rights. He worked diligently for artists' rights to manage their own creative output, and he spoke out against the corporate methods of the music industry and the constraints that artists experience in the commercial music world.

Petty was noted for his personal integrity and commitment to his family and friends, in addition to his music and activism. He was a loving husband, father, and friend, and his kindness, generosity, and compassion will be remembered by all who knew him.

Tom Petty's status as one of the finest artists in the history of rock and roll music remains safe as time passes. His music continues to inspire and unite people all across the world, and his influence on the industry and the lives of those who knew him personally will be remembered forever.

CONCLUSION

The book "Tom Petty Biography: Uncovering the Life and Passion of a Rock Star" provides readers with an in-depth and all-encompassing look at the life and legacy of one of the most important rock performers in the history of the genre. The reader has had the opportunity throughout this biography to look into Tom Petty's early years, his ascent to stardom, and the different hardships and victories he had in his personal life as well as his work.

Tom Petty is unquestionably regarded as one of the most important figures in the history of rock music due to his undying love of music and his unrelenting drive to create and perform. His classic music, which he recorded both with the Heartbreakers and on his own as a solo artist, has moved the emotions of millions of people and will continue to do so for future generations. This biography sheds light not only on his exceptional talent but also on his tenacity, humility, and compassion, all of which contributed to the fact that he was a genuine inspiration to a great number of artists as well as fans.

As we consider the life of Tom Petty, we come to realize the significant influence he had not only on the field of music but also on the lives of those who were fortunate enough to know him. His life serves as a powerful example of the transformative potential of unwavering commitment, the life-changing significance of being one's authentic self, and the undaunted tenacity that lives within each of us.

The documentary "Tom Petty: Uncovering the Life and Passion of a Rock Star" is a fitting homage to an outstanding musician as well as a remarkable man. Hoping that this book will serve as a source of motivation for future generations, encouraging them to go for their goals with the same zeal and commitment that Tom Petty showed throughout his extraordinary life. Tom Petty, may you now rest in peace knowing that the people whose lives you touched will always keep your music and your spirit alive.

Printed in Great Britain
by Amazon

33020247R00024